CW01624215

Peter Handke, who was born in Griffen, Austria, in 1942 and studied law at the University of Graz, published his first novel in 1966, the same year as his first play was staged in Frankfurt. This play, **Offending the Audience**, was not seen in London until 1971 but was followed by productions of **My Foot My Tutor** in 1971, **Self Accusation, Prophecy** and **Calling For Help** in 1972, **Kaspar** and **The Ride Across Lake Constance** in 1973, the latter transferring successfully to the West End, and **They Are Dying Out**, staged by the National Theatre in 1976. **The Long Way Round** was first performed in English by the National Theatre in 1989.

Of his novels, **The Goalie's Anxiety at the Penalty Kick** (subsequently made into an award-winning film) and **Short Letter, Long Farewell** were published in Britain in 1977, as was the semi-autobiographical book **A Sorrow Beyond Dreams**. In 1980 came **The Left-Handed Woman**, a novel drawn from his film of the same title, which he directed himself, in 1985 the trilogy of thematically connected novels, **Slow Homecoming**, in 1986 his novel **Across** and in 1988 **Repetition**.

The photograph of Peter Handke on the back cover was taken by Jerry Bauer.

BY THE SAME AUTHOR

PLAYS

Offending the Audience and Self-Accusation

Kaspar

The Ride Across Lake Constance

They Are Dying Out

My Foot My Tutor (in *Shakespeare the Sadist and other plays* by Bauer, Fassbinder, Handke and Kroetz)

NOVELS

The Goalie's Anxiety at the Penalty Kick

Short Letter, Long Farewell

A Sorrow Beyond Dreams

The Left-Handed Woman

Slow Homecoming

Across

Repetition

PETER HANDKE

The Long Way Round

A dramatic poem

Translated by Ralph Manheim

Methuen Drama

A Methuen Modern Play

First published in Great Britain in 1989 by Methuen Drama,
Michelin House, 81 Fulham Road, London SW3 6RB
Copyright © Suhrkamp Verlag Frankfurt am Main 1981
English translation copyright © Ralph Manheim 1989

Printed in Great Britain
by Richard Clay Ltd, Bungay, Suffolk

A CIP catalogue record for this book is available
from the British Library

ISBN 0 413 62440 4

Caution

All rights in this play are strictly reserved

This book is sold subject to the condition
that it shall not, by way of trade or otherwise,
be lent, resold, hired out or otherwise circulated
without the publisher's prior consent in any form
of binding or cover other than that in which
it is published and without a similar condition
including this condition being imposed
on the subsequent purchaser.

Characters

NOVA

GREGOR

THE CARETAKER of the dormitory

HANS, Gregor's brother

ANTON, IGNATZ, ALBIN — Hans's workmates

SOPHIE, Gregor's sister

OLD WOMAN

HANS'S CHILD

'A tender slowness is the tempo of these words.'
Friedrich Nietzsche, *Ecce Homo*

'Rolling on the river . . .'
Creedence Clearwater Revival, *Proud Mary*

For the actors:

'Here stand *I*'
– All are in the right –
After the final words go on playing –
Fervid irony.

I

GREGOR *in front of the curtain.* NOVA *comes out and points at him.*

NOVA. He had no ears for the underground chorus of the homesick. Man from overseas, blind to the drops of blood in the snow spectator's mask on his cheeks, hand among straphangers' hands wanderer without shadow – lord of the northsoutheastwest. That's all I can think of just now.

GREGOR. I've had a letter from my brother. It's about money and more than money, about the house of our dead parents and the land it's on. Being the eldest, I've inherited both. He asks me to waive my claim to the house and land, so our sister can set herself up in business. My sister works in a department store. My brother learned a trade, but for years now he has been working on construction projects far from our home and village. The jobs he does there have nothing to do with the trade he originally learned –

It's a long story. I can't remember a single moment when I definitely loved my brother and sister, but I remember hours and hours of fear and worry on their account. Once, before they were even old enough to go to school, they disappeared for a whole day. I looked for them all along the brook, past the next village to the place where it empties into the river. I may not have known exactly what to do with them, but it was always a comfort to know that they were somewhere around the house. We were often at loggerheads, but always reconciled by the thought that at least we were all there together. Later, I wanted the other two to stay on at school as I had done. Often on my way back to the university, I'd pass the sawmill and see my brother in his blue work clothes; this was his first job. And then in the bus I'd ride past the village shop, where I knew my sister in her apprentice's smock would be handling bolts of cloth or working in the cold storeroom at the back, and I'd feel a pang that was something more than the usual homesickness. I'll do something, I thought. But over the years I spent away from the village my brother and sister faded away. I formed other attachments; you, for instance. I didn't see anything wrong with that. My family meant no more to me than distant voices in the snow. Just once I felt closer to one of them. One night on television there was a story about a teenage girl who was ostracised in her village because she had been raped. In the end she killed herself. She wrapped herself in a veil, or maybe it was a shawl, and lay down on the sloping riverbank. She started rolling, but she kept getting caught in the bushes or the tall grass, and sometimes the slope wasn't steep enough. But she made it in the end. She fell plop into the water and sank like a stone. When the organ music started up, I burst into tears. After that I felt better. The room I was in that night was large and light. The message the drowning girl brought home to me had to do with my brother. It commanded me to take him, for a time at least, out of the house and away from the village, which he had never once left, and show him something of the outside world. Once at least, I decided, he must get away from his work and put on something different from his blue work clothes, and glimpse the radiance of the cities. Up until then the only town known to him was the nearby provincial capital, and even of that he knew no more than what he could see from his bed in the hospital for work accidents. He was hardly more than a boy, but his arms and legs were as scarred and mutilated as if he had been through a war. He accepted my invitation meekly enough. Nothing much came of it. Still, it was something in his life. But in the years that followed, we quarrelled. I couldn't forgive him for the worry and grief he caused our parents – a lot worse than most village boys. In the end I put him out of the house. We had a scene. I was in the doorway and he was in front of the house next door, on the boundary of our land. Between us a suitcase full of his belongings, which I had put there that morning when he came back from one of his escapades. Silence in the house behind me, which only a moment before had been full of my mother's soundless moaning about her son. I shouted at my brother: 'If you ever dare to set foot in this house again, I'll shoot you.' He just laughed. There was no gun in the house and the only thing I'd ever shot at was plastic flowers in a shooting gallery. He shouted back: 'You just come out here and I'll knock you dead.' We both stood our ground, I on the steps of the house, he on the boundary of our land, exchanging threats and curses. That night he actually did pick up his bag and vanish across the border. He went to work on some construction project and lived in some workers' dormitory on the outskirts of some big city. Nevertheless, it seemed to me later on that our battle scene was a fraud, an act we put on. Several times, while we were still exchanging insults, I thought of laughing and making up. At any moment we could have stopped and gone out for a beer. In spite of all the harm my brother had done, I wasn't really angry with him, not even in the thick of battle. I suppose it was just a game we had to play. There was nothing final about it. He kept coming up in my dreams. Our meeting at our parents' graveside didn't bring reconciliation, but it did confirm and reinforce the old tie between us. From then on it was certain that we would never again exchange an angry word. I knew that I might have done far worse things than he had, if I hadn't by some stroke of luck escaped from the life that had been mapped out for me. My brother loves his wife and child as his saviours. The house has become his last refuge. He doesn't ever want to leave it. He asked me to let him stay there for the rest of his life. That day at the graveyard I saw the old scamp as a proud man, though a stranger to our village. It wasn't so much a look as a smell, and that smell is still with me. His letter on my sister's behalf puzzles me. And then again it doesn't, because when we embraced that day I also smelled self-sacrifice.

NOVA. You started talking about your brother and sister. But so far you've spoken only of him.

GREGOR. My sister was the most inoffensive, the least mysterious of us three. She wasn't a typical shopgirl. When I looked in on her at the village shop, or later in the department store, she made the impression of an assistant, or possibly a friend, of the real, official saleswoman. Beside her, my sister seemed unconcerned, untouched by responsibility. She didn't dislike selling, but she did it without passion or enthusiasm. Her handwriting on sales slips was still that of a child. The fact is that she never wanted to be anything more than an underling. I've never felt at all sorry for her. But there's one thing I've never forgotten, the way shop owners or supervisors looked at my sister when she wasted her time in conversation with me, a non-customer. I felt as if the daylight had been switched off. There was nothing left but flashing steel rods, rows of different-coloured dresses, plastic carpeting, musty wardrobe smell, dead, dyed hair, and meat-coloured fingernails. One day I noticed that my sister had become hunchbacked and I wanted to get her out of there. But how? And where to? I didn't think her capable of independence. A shop in this day and age? Well, perhaps if some ancestor could be there in spirit to help her. But in a remodelled shop, even in the creakiest, crankiest old premises, wouldn't everything be an imitation of the department store? And yet, wasn't it I who gave my sister the idea of setting herself up on her own by suggesting that she should get out of her profession and class, not necessarily into something higher, just so she got out. A mortgage now would give her a chance. But it's not just indecision on my part. I feel guilty. As if I'd talked my sister out of a job that gave her security if nothing else, and in so doing endangered my brother's hope of coming into the house and land that he certainly needs more than anyone else. You see, I've given up the house for lost; you'll never find a head for business in a race of paupers. And that's not all. I can't forget that it's our parents' house. They built it almost unaided and it took several years off their lives. The land bore fruit thanks to the work of their hands. They encased a spring in rock and brought the water to the house and garden in long underground pipes. Have you any idea what that means? Terrace walls were built with the stones cleared from the land. And on that land trees are now growing, or in places just grass, but every little corner of the property has a name of its own. For years the place didn't mean much to me. You told me once how every time you visited your first home a feeling of bliss came over you before you'd even arrived. I understood, and I envied you. I couldn't have said that about myself. But since I got that letter, the old place has come to life for me. That's where most of my dreams happen, the terrifying as well as the golden ones. A tree on the uppermost terrace marks the centre of the property. From there you can look south across the border. That puts the tree in the other country. A broad plain, humped by terminal moraines, extends from there to the frontier mountain. It's empty and quiet in the dusk, the humps smoke, the glaciers have just melted away, it's ten thousand years before our time, and it *is* our time. I had secretly set aside the terrace with the tree on it for myself. I thought I'd live there later on, in a wooden house, parts of which I could actually describe. Believe me, it's a beautiful place. I don't mean only the house and grounds; there's the soil, too, a livelihood. I've seen the crowned snake there, the heraldic animal of the place. I don't want that house to become a house of mourning. I see our parents' creation – yes, creation – going under. I see every peasant's hovel in every God-forsaken village turned into a bank or a supermarket or an office block, and around those office blocks the country has vanished. I see no lonely paths, I see no way out to the open plain. I see my irresponsibility and my betrayal. Now I know that I can't do a thing for my brother and sister, or for anyone else. The most I can do is preserve. And that I will do, preserve at all costs. I'd like best to leave the letter unanswered and stay here with the one thing I can be faithful to – my work, which is endangered in any case. But now you will tell me what to do.

NOVA. Play the game. Endanger your work still more. Don't be a protagonist. Invite confrontation. But keep away from purposes. Avoid ulterior motives. Conceal nothing. Be soft and be strong. Be crafty. Commit yourself but despise victory. Don't observe, don't scrutinise, but be on the lookout for signs. Be vulnerable. Show your eyes. Lure other people into the depths, give yourself elbow room and consider each man in his own image. Make no decisions without enthusiasm. Don't let failure worry you. Above all, have time, go out of your way. Let yourself be diverted. Take holidays, so to speak. Listen to what every tree and every brook has to say. Stop off where you feel like it, enjoy the sunshine. Forget your family, encourage strangers. Bend down to look at trifles, escape into wilderness, despise the drama of fate, ignore misfortune, laugh at conflict. Show your colours until you are in the right and the rustling of the leaves sounds sweet in your ears. Take the long way round. I will follow you.

They go out to the right and left.

2

First set. In the background a section of a large but deserted construction site, half hidden by a hessian curtain. In the middleground a large shack, the workers' dormitory. In the empty foreground an old woman, who is THE CARETAKER *of the shack, and* GREGOR. *Clear sunset light, which does not change.*

THE CARETAKER. You're in luck. This is a good day. The building here is almost finished. Next week the men start work on another project in the next valley. Most have already moved. Your brother and a few others have stayed to put on the finishing touches. They will be here soon, they're going to celebrate. I haven't put the beer on ice. They've all got delicate kidneys. This whole valley is draughty. There used to be a forest where we are now. I come from around here. The workers are all from somewhere else. At weekends I've always been alone here, guarding the shack. It can be awfully quiet on Sundays. You can hear the bells from the village. I used to read a lot. Now I switch on the radio or the telly, it's soothing. The builder put in a television set. But I'm glad Monday morning when the boys come back from their homes. For two years we've been living here together. Soon they'll dismantle the shack and reassemble it in the next valley. They won't be taking me with them, I'll go back to my village. I've still got my little room there and I'll get myself a cat. It's an old village. The church is on a little rocky hill. Only now it's closed most of the time. But soon there will be a dog show on the village square. Oh these times. I'm fond of your brother. But some think he's a good-for-nothing, and sometimes he seems to think so too. As a rule he works harder than the others, like a wild man. But then he slips away and hides, and they practically have to go looking for him. The foremen think he's unreliable, more than once they've threatened to dismiss him. I happen to know that he's not lazy, only restless. Your brother is the only one of the whole lot who still, after all these years, minds being away from home. When he stares into space, he doesn't see emptiness, he sees pictures. He is the bravest and strongest of them all, but he's also the most unstable and in need of help, the most to be pitied. Yet sometimes he's the life and soul of the party, and it's him that sings the loudest. By the time the building here is officially opened, the builders will be working on the next project, and I'll be trotting down the village street with a tin pail, getting milk for myself and my cat. Who will hear my voice then? Oh, these times.

GREGOR. I've come a long way. As soon as I entered the valley, clouds of dust were blowing from all the many construction sites. They made the river water muddy. Behind every signboard indicating the name of a village I saw a bigger signboard marked with the number of a construction project. But then I took the high road through the orchards. I could see the dust clouds on the opposite slope, mingled with sand thrown up by columns of trucks. Sometimes the light was a sulphurous yellow; little by little it got to be right, a kind of beauty spreading from the distance. I saw only one passer-by, a man in a black suit, on his way home from a funeral. And down in the valley I saw gravediggers in bright-coloured waistcoats with silver buttons, and I heard the scraping of their shovels, louder than the rumbling of the trucks on the opposite slope and the rustling of the leaves on mine. Yes, I've seen the coming and going of the days, and now I can say: When this building is finished and all the dust holes have been sealed up, your countryside will be new again. Follow the eyes of your cat when they escape the concrete walls and look into space. Out there the water trembles in a leaf-lined pothole; the tremor comes back to you with the force of a heartbeat and you raise your arms in amazement. In a twinkling perhaps your valley will be old again, and the concrete arches will be component forms of remotest antiquity. On my way here I passed any number of dark caves; mightn't this building soon be a part of that system of caves? Mightn't concrete revert to primal rock? There are springs in construction debris, they will carve out new valleys in the slope. The country, I thought, is still beautiful; it will be all right. Let the motor cars roam around in it like Frankenstein's monsters. Once I was caught in a snow storm. The snow got so deep I began to be afraid, but then I noticed all the quiet things around me. While heavy branches crashed to the ground, flakes piled up peacefully in the forks of trees, and the dark spots in the snowfield were lime blossoms. Isn't there a proverb around here that goes: 'Children run under the wind'? So don't say: O these times! Say: O Time! (*He stops.*) But will I be able to believe tomorrow what I know today?

THE CARETAKER. No one has ever wasted a word on the country around here. When I was young, our village people talked a lot about a sculptor who was supposed to have grown up there in the last century. Today there's not a child in the village who ever heard of him, but in those days he was the secret hero of the whole valley. Every time I passed the house where he was born, I felt proud that someone had come from the same village as the rest of us. His statues stopped people from running off to the city. His house looked so big and spacious. It was still lived in and kept up, a cottage like all the others in the level, monotonous row, yet it was quieter than the others and seemed taller. To me the sculptor was life itself, the living man-child. He stood for all seven ages, especially the first. At times I was his double; his resurrection; as a child, I was the child-sculptor, new-born, walking the village streets with worldwide eyes. O . . . yes, I as I sit here, an old woman, caretaker of the workers' dormitory. Such things exist, and never forget it. They are real. In the morning mists, the parallel struts of the hayrack were arrows aimed at the sunrise. In the autumn, the apples on the leafless trees were glowing billiard balls. Crossed sheaves of corn formed our feudal community tent. In the dusk the brook flowed over bright stone signposts, shimmering cliffs rose up from the plain, that was the hour of the imagination, space ships came gliding down, and the sculptor was everywhere, all over the countryside. He brought unity; set his imprint on the whole valley; breathed upon me, poor insignificant soul; wrapped me in the cloak of innocence, which even the inveterate schnapps drinker you see before you has never ceased to feel on her shoulders as the opposite of a burden. It's perfectly normal, get that into your heads, you slaves of facts. How desolate our valleys are today. Did you notice that the high road you took is an educational walk for visitors, that every variety of tree has a label on it and that similar labels identify the old wayside shrines as 'places of worship', rather than 'larches' or 'beeches'. How desolate I feel most of the time – without my familiar surroundings. Bells – people used to say – don't tell time; they put us in mind of eternity. Nowadays they tell nothing and put us in mind of nothing – big clappers, air-displacing cast iron, beastly, tinny noise. Dogs come running into the churches and drink up the holy water. And no one takes an interest in the place any more. So much goes on that is worth handing down, even here at the construction site – but no one records anything and nothing is passed on. Once in a while somebody digs a curious root out of the rubble, takes it home, varnishes it, and uses it as a garden ornament. Down with you root carvers, I say, and down with flowers grown in worn-out wheelbarrows and empty dog kennels. Wilderness, where art thou? The newspapers mention us now and then when there's been an accident or a crime. That, at least, is something; take my word for it, we read every word of those stories, the name of the village flashes up at us as if it were our own. A fellow came here once with a tape recorder and a camera; he commiserated with us in the name of his readers and expected us to feel sorry for ourselves. But that's not how we want to be mentioned. We want to be praised. Or better still: let them glorify our countryside with its forms and colours. Unknown master of the big construction sites, where are you? Take your daily walks here in our mud, justify our activity by your works, make it possible to invoke the things here and proclaim their names. For nowhere, far and wide, is there any thing that can be invoked or any name that can be proclaimed. Ubi est domus dei in qua invocabitur nomen eius?

The WORKERS *from the construction site enter through a gap in the hessian curtain. They are dressed in different shades of more or less faded blue. They take off their yellow hard hats. They are* HANS, GREGOR*'s brother, and three others. The others disappear at once into the dormitory.* THE CARETAKER *does likewise.* HANS *walks around the dormitory. He looks at* GREGOR, *then takes a step back and swings his outstretched arm to right and left and up and down. Silence; or possibly from the shack muffled sounds of steps, dishes, the radio.*

HANS. I recognised you in the distance by your posture. Our parents used to say about you: 'He looks like he doesn't understand a thing' and it's still true. But then again, I know it's not true. You're shrewd. You always knew what was going to happen, you looked ahead. With you I never knew where I was. You beat me at every game. You didn't cheat but you were usually a cruel winner, at least with your brother and sister. You'd sit there looking like somebody who'd won a game. You never got the better of us graciously, then your triumph could have been admired. A good victory, says our proverb, brings happiness to the vanquished. But you seldom failed to humiliate us when we lost. It didn't matter much to me, but our sister was a poor loser. Even after a slight defeat, she couldn't go on playing. It made her so angry that she wept and bawled, and you'd laugh at her. Remember? There were times when she'd lock herself in, and you'd run after her and go on making fun of her outside the locked door? Was it only when playing games that you were like that? No, it was all the time. Many a time when you were needed, you weren't there. Our parents were always complaining about it. He's only interested in himself, they said, he doesn't care about anyone else. He's full of compassion, but in the long run, he can't abide people's weaknesses. And then you'd come around and you'd be every inch our brother. Get a load of that, we'd say, it's our brother. He's a bit different from us, but he's one of us all the same. He's like us and he'll never forget us. No one believed me when I said you'd come here to this wilderness and now you're really here. (*The brothers embrace.* HANS *goes into the dormitory to change his clothes.*)

GREGOR *briefly alone. He walks slowly up and down, first hanging his head, then looking up. He stands still and looks around. Now the light is on in the dormitory. The hessian curtain is ruffled, giving an impression of blowing. From then on the breeze remains audible.* GREGOR *raises both arms.* HANS *comes out of the shack with three others, stops on the platform in front of it and points down at his brother.* THE WORKERS *have exchanged their blue work clothes for after-hours dress. Washed, shaved, and combed, they seem extraordinarily clean, self-possessed, and dignified as well as adventurous and daring.*

HANS. That's my brother you're looking at. I was less than a year old when he left a gate open that had been built just for me. I fell down the stairs and bumped my head on the cement floor. After that, so they said, I wasn't fit to be anything better than a worker. When he was sent on errands, he took the two of us, his brother and sister, along. He'd sit down by the roadside and read and read. The two of us didn't know the way home by ourselves, so we stood there weeping and wailing, but he never let that interfere with his reading. Later on, when he was supposed to help us with our homework, he'd just stand over us and hit us on the head. When our tears fell on the ink, he'd tear the pages out of our exercise books. And nobody dared punish him. The whole house, the whole village, were afraid of him, because that was the way he was. He drove us into the woods to pick blueberries, and he refused to understand that we weren't as eager to fill the baskets as he was; we'd sit in the bushes and sulk and he'd insult us, lazy animals he called us. For every blow and every insult I swore I'd get even. I seldom had the feeling that he was fond of us. He didn't show it until he was far away. His letters were more than messages of greeting, they showed real interest. It didn't dawn on me until much later that he wanted us to be like himself. He was alone and he took himself for the norm. But we're different. I'm a worker. Believe me, I was born to be a worker. I don't want to be like him. I don't long to eat what he eats or drink what he drinks. People often ask me if I envy him. My answer is that I'm content to be a worker. All the same, he's trustworthy. He's not some tramp with a tape recorder, who steals the story and secret of your life. Maybe he has his own way of listening to you. But he's one of us, he scratches himself in the same places. (*All step forward.* HANS *introduces the others.*) We're all from the same valley. This one is Anton. He lives at the end of the valley. On Monday morning he picks us up in his car, one after the other. If you ride through the empty villages at dawn, long before the first bus starts up, and you see one man, and then another, and another, standing muffled and silent by the roadside holding a seabag or a thick briefcase with a thermos sticking out of it; that's us. Anton is building his house right now. At weekends I go and help him. The water pipes have been put in, the cellar has been dug. In a year the frame ought to be finished; in another year there ought to be a room on the ground floor, and little by little we'll build on to it. Anton was a long time overseas. Take a look at him. He's your age and he has hardly any teeth left. 'We love you just as you are.' Our wives are obliging enough to talk like that, but naturally they'd be glad if we were different. Just as we would be glad to have them – oh yes! – with bosoms and without varicose veins. Don't our names for each other sound as if we were talking to our parents? 'Father,' my wife says to me. 'Mother,' I say to my wife. And yet only yesterday a night together was as hot and viscous as the magma, the open fields around us were like a great dance floor that we had all to ourselves, the sky above us was like a warm breathing inside us, and the universe was a light breeze with us tucked away inside it. We're all of us still young. Anton slaved for years overseas, in the far north, laying a pipeline, but wasn't he in your class at the village school? Here (*he points*) you see his frozen ear, which the teacher threatened only yesterday to pull off. Here (*he points*) the crushed fingertips, which belonged only yesterday to the hand of the boy in front of me in the First Communion procession – too short of finger to hold the thick ritual candle, still dripping with holy water. And here (*he points at the background*) the rumbling of the concrete mixers, day after day, yet no more present than the crackling of the Easter bonfire twenty years ago; the daily smell of steaming tar in our nostrils but on the palms of our hands the far stronger smell of early apples stolen in orchards long ago; the shouting of the foremen and engineers on this construction job drowned by the gentle sound of a house pet long ago getting up or lying down in a region removed from clock time. This isn't a so-called memory. We're still young – Here you see Ignatz. (*He points.*) He too worked a long time overseas. Not far from the Equator. He's from the village next to ours, and he has gone back to live there. He lives alone, he has no family. If you pass through his village, you'll suddenly come to the shell of a castle, built of concrete blocks. The towers and battlements are unfinished; he is the builder and architect. He works on it mostly in the winter, our slack season; he's looking forward to his retirement; then he'll finish his house. Ignatz (*he points*) wears a truss; sometimes, when he's carrying a concrete block his guts stick out. He gets delirious at night, then he imitates jungle cries in his sleep. His castle is next door to a peasant's cottage and it's not much bigger; behind it there's a kitchen garden; in the garden there's a wooden shed, and in the shed there's a straw tick, a bench, and a sawdust stove. The man you see here, weak in the knees after his day in the mud and rubble, oozing with snot and coughing up phlegm, is honoured in his village. At the pub there's a collection box for him and his castle. People put in coins which add up to quite a sum at the end of the month. The castle is a strange building. It tapers to a point at the top and under the full moon it fits into the great pyramidal mountain behind it. This picture is his only reason for building the castle; otherwise he'd have no use for it. In the shack, though, he pins a new collection of naked women to the wall beside his bed every Monday; in the canteen (*he points*) he's always the first to sit down to lunch and the last to leave the table. If at night, when the lights are out and the radio closes down, you hear a monumental glugging in the darkness, it's sure to be the lord of his castle, the saint, the man from overseas, drinking tequila. And while he drinks he says: 'Construction site, valley, country, earth below, and stars above, listen; it's me.' But hurrah for the nutcases, even if they're only pretending, because this is our last night here. And hurrah for the savages, even if they are mere ghosts: for tomorrow we'll be sitting at home in our kitchen–living room, winding all the alarm clocks. (*He turns around in a ring with* IGNATZ.) Great spirit of the universe, come down to us today, unfold, unfold in the spacious sky, let us hover a while above the ground, lift up our innermost lungs like parachutes. New life, show us your resplendent face time and again above the bristling antennas, behind the swaying treetops, in the midst of greening thickets, in the glazed eyes of our fellow men, between the cracks in the drifting clouds. Don't leave us alone with the artificial vibration of our short-lived machines – or else electronic bombast will soon envelop the whole earth in darkness. Don't relegate the dear, good, enduring things to a dream world, but disclose them in broad daylight, put them into the sunlight at our heads, both far and near, and open us up now and then to the quintessential tree, the quintessential river, to the shimmering mountain ridge where the gods live, to the early aeroplanes that we call clouds, to the flower, that sheltering chalice. Tonight let us be what we are – men of a primordial age. Shape the moon behind the branches, the snail shells in the mud, and the iron rods in the concrete into a unity with the tongues in our mouths. Country, put away your flag and your emblems. Valleys all, drop your anthems, forget your names; paths leading to this place, hide yourselves in namelessness. (*He walks the length of the stage.*) And you, construction site, come to life in nameless simplicity. Let this place (*he points*) be nameless tonight. Let it be called 'Wilderness', and let no one be here but us. We too are nameless. (*To all those in the circle.*) When you answer, remember, you are unknown. Show no one your home. Forget the verdict and stay away from the trial. Don't look at people – there's nothing more to be seen. Move without music – music leads in the wrong direction. Only the softest murmur is in tune with human hearing. (*The silence of transformation.*) Names are falling away. We are in the open. Now, once again, we can say 'earth' to this place – This man is ordinarily called Albin. At home he lives in a cellar. The bosses here think he's retarded, they hire him only for a month at a time. Once at the restaurant the waitress sat down with him, you (*to* GREGOR) should have seen the way he clutched her hand. The way he squeezed it. She didn't just cry, she didn't just laugh, she screamed and sobbed. A couple of times he tugged at her apron strings and grinned from ear to ear. Back here in the shack he kept saying: 'Wasn't it sweet the way she sat down with me?' Albin isn't an idiot. Of course not. He just pretends to be stupid if he doesn't know you. In the main he doesn't want to know anybody. If he lives in his cellar, it's by choice. He built it for war. It's his bunker, but we can use it too. Maybe we'll be glad to have it before long. I've often been there, I've even spent the night there. There's a radio in one corner, it buzzes and knocks and wheezes, and sometimes there are voices from across the sea, from island to island. A bird means twilight. A flock of pigeons means dawn. This cellar branches out in all directions and there's more than canned goods in it. In every wall there's a niche for stones and fossils. Every niche stands for a different construction site, and each specimen is labelled, but never with the standard name. Albin is also the man who bellows in deserted railway stations at night. He is the man with the switchblade knife, the man with the car horn, who flings a jug at the glass cabinet over the bar and rams his head into the stomach of some innocent bystander. He's the grinning killer with the death's head. He's the uniformed policeman at political demos, who sees all civilians as enemies. In the middle of peacetime he cracks nut shells as if he'd volunteered for the firing squad. Albin is a jailbird. In every building he knows the emergency exit. He sits in porn cinemas and stinks. He plonks himself down beside you in an empty bus and whistles all through the ride between his tooth stumps. At night he runs across the moors, screaming blue murder. He takes a string bag and goes shopping for his paralysed mother. The inscription on his tombstone says 'Missing'. He is also a woman. If you touch him, he screeches: 'Don't tickle me!' When playing football, he stands between the goalposts; he specialises in high balls and misses all the low ones. When he goes to a wake, he sits up all night with the mourners. In the woods he steps out of the clefts in hollow tree trunks. He walks in the middle of the Roman road with his divining rod. His dog deposits sticky slobber on your Sunday trousers. He creeps into the undergrowth with a stick of dynamite in his mouth. He is blue and yellow. An enormous bull is standing on his tongue, that's why he can't talk. He has lain with you under a heart. He appears to you as a face in the clouds. His last picture is oval, black and white, and his dented bicycle is lying in the grass beside the milestone. His distinguishing marks are this wasted thigh muscle (*he points*), caused by long lying in the hospital, and a stiff knee – a professional error, doctors aren't interested in the likes of us. Who is he? He's a riddle. (*To* GREGOR.) And heaven help you if you tell anyone who he is. And heaven help you if you dare to guess who we are. One word of interpretation and the festival is over. The festival consists in devising the riddle. Maybe we are the exploited, the insulted and injured, the salt of the earth. But we often get up at night. We like to piss on the soft concrete. Occasionally we look out of the corners of our eyes and see the circling of the stars. We shout at the waitress: 'Come here or I'll bite you.' We make soup out of Oxo cubes on a hot plate. At night we put on our National Health glasses and study the Scriptures. We try to kiss reluctant women and miss our aim. We wear ties when serving as marriage witnesses. We fall off scaffolds and break both our heels. We collect travel, danger, and dirt premiums and slaughter a pig for the winter. We godfather each other's children and bear each other's palls. But we're not friends. Each one of us lies alone with his face to the partition; all night we sense the breathing of our mate, lying in the next cubicle with his face to the partition. In the morning when the first alarm clock goes off, we switch on the light and the radio without so much as a good morning, we smoke our first cigarette in our underpants, scratch the frost flowers off the windows, curse the north wind, the frozen ground, and the snow, and drink our Nescafé. By the middle of the week we get restless and start masturbating, but the wind is too cold out here. In the afternoon, which is the longest part of the working day, we think of our one and only friend, who has had an accident or is off in some foreign country, wish our mates dead, get more and more careless at our work, and possibly get killed. At home we've become too stupid for our children, their voices and movements get on our nerves; we send them to bed early, go down on our knees to our wives on the kitchen linoleum, rest our heads on their laps, and tell them about our undying hatred of the bosses and our eternal loneliness, get the tears out of our system, and slip away to the bar. Day after day, we say to one another: We'll have to stick it out for another few years. The earth will have to stagger around a few more times before we're able to go at last, once and for all, from house to tree, from tree to road, from road to village, and from village back home again. A few more of us will have to be crippled by work accidents before they stop calling us 'malingerers'. A few years, a few decades. But even if we're not friends, we are waiting together, time and again we assert our existence as riddles, and none of you exploiters of opinions and behaviour patterns can see us. We are the figures crossing the fields in the distance, the silhouettes in the inter-city bus riding over the snow-covered plain. Our shadowy faces fill the underground train from end to end, we lose sight of one another for barely a moment on the curves. Sometimes we speak to the distant mountains, and sometimes we even manage to be on the horizon, to be a ravine or a cliff in the blue between two mountains. Once a day perhaps, we are an answering sign deep down in the grass, or a sun lamp in the middle of a thicket, or a nest of light in a copper beech, or the sheltering darkness inside a yew tree. At any time we can be the rootwind, which suddenly rises from under the treetops, the murmur of the days and nights, the infinite green, the shimmering smooth sea, the *galéné* of the proverb. Tomorrow perhaps we shall be nothing. The day after tomorrow we shall be eight feet under and not even a footnote in the history books. But time and again we shall be remembered by the white cloud-graves high overhead. We are the fatherless, the acquitted, the exiled and alienated, the beautiful strangers, the great unknowns, the meaningfully slow, the people of all times. That is our way of using the force of mystery. Today we embody the craft we have actually learned, the practitioners of which were formerly known as the common people. But let's drop the hype for now. A people creates itself after all. What do we care if our bosses live near enough to the job to allow them to go home every night. Let them push their lawnmowers back and forth in front of their houses with their pretentious arcades, just as they did yesterday. See them now in rubber gloves, washing the mud off their tyres, while indoors their wives, likewise in rubber gloves, wash the mud off their rubber boots. See the architect coming up from the cellar with a bottle in hand, see him showing his visitor, the solicitor, the date on the label, while in the adjoining room the architect's wife puts the solicitor's wife on to the new butcher she has just discovered, who does the most marvellous saddle of venison, or the new baker, who makes the most astonishing weight-reducing tidbits. (*The others act out the scene.*) Yum, yum. And see their children sitting there with downcast eyes, the little darlings, who have everything and love nothing, have seen everything and take nothing seriously, who have always been privileged to see, hear, read, and touch beautiful things but are utterly incapable of appreciating, admiring, and revering anything whatever, who, when they grow up, are quick to tell the story of their unhappy, loveless childhoods, and proceed to hand down and perpetuate their heritage of lovelessness. See the pampered man and wife putting on a record after an evening at the theatre or in front of the television, letting the slavish machine serve up caressing scraps of the humanly possible or even the great things they might supposedly have done, but never never will do. Yum, yum. And now see our pampered pair climbing the stairs like mourners without coffin or bereavement, see the ladies and gentlemen embrace as they did yesterday and the day before, without needing one another, without tears in their eyes, without grief, without enthusiasm; see them lie together without conferring release. See them satisfied, without satisfaction. See how easy they sleep, failing to suspect that this has been a parting for ever. Yum, yum, yum. Yes, they have been recognised. The powerful today are the disenchanted. For years they have had no secrets. They drift with the crowd. But no river flows with them. They think they are moving, but no cloud moves with them. They never stop playing, but no amount of playing can make them children again. They join in our festivities but we keep away from theirs. Only we the injured hear beauty and see into the distance. *They* are without mystery, the noisy dead. As the saying goes: 'Evil is quick to invent its own machines' – they are the machines of evil. Tonight we are having a different kind of festivity. (*He calls into the shack.*) Hey, Mother Construction Site. No musical accompaniment tonight. No artificially amplified voices. No gogglebox to disfigure the clear night. Come. We will celebrate the hour when our hands are as free as gods. Tear yourself away from your crossword. Pour the booze down the drain. Turn the calendar to the wall. Switch off the telly, shut out the false images. Get away from the cloud that yields no drinking water and steer clear of the barren waves. Fold up the antenna and hide the bloodless box under a white crocheted napkin inscribed with the legend: 'Down with blue light in living rooms!' Hey, Mother Construction Site. Stop the loose mouths. Keep the radio quiet. Pierce the soundproof wall, risk the moonshot out of deafdumbblindness, and glide down to us in this playful, refreshing at-homeness that sets all things to right. (*Little by little, the noise has died down in the dormitory. Though it was never more than background noise, the stillness now is striking. In it one can hear the music of the spheres.*) Hey, Mother Construction Site. While there's still light, look at yourself. Seek out your eyes. A field, a star. Irradiate your look of suffering, turn your forehead into a diadem, quiver anew, step out of the shack, and scream the first scream.

(*The light goes out in the shack.* THE CARETAKER *appears on the platform, ageless, transformed, without particular ornament, in no particular attitude, radiantly beautiful. She smiles with closed lips, but does nothing else of the kind, only lets herself be quietly looked at, while she herself looks at something else.*)

Surprisingly, ALBIN *begins to sing – not a normal singing, but a singsong, not loud but full-voiced.*

ALBIN.

Stepped out of jail and went to the bar for a
beer
it wasn't there and it wasn't here
The man in the storeroom said 'Take the
midnight train'
That's just what I did and I can't complain
I came to the river with time to spare
eleven thousand women were standing there
St Ursula leaned over and said to me
'The Beast awaits us all in the northern territory'
I slept on my feet and had a fall
the bus driver didn't like that at all
He said: 'Tell your mother to look us up'
and his face turned as yellow as a buttercup.
I lay in the grass and dreamed of snow
the black stag-beetle pinched my toe
The boathouse lady said: 'Come here'
The back seat was empty, nothing to fear
After a while I lost the thread
the valley ended, my heartbeat pounded in my
head
'This road just doubles back,' I shouted at the sky
An iceberg hit me in the eye
Out of the window I jumped with a shout
The light wasn't on and the light wasn't out
The pilot turned round to me and said:
'Hey, Albin. Better go home and dance the
polka of St Dunderhead'

But on the way I lost a shoe
I said to my heart: 'Shut up, you nuisance
        you'
Then who came down the road, eating a chunk
        of meat
but old man Ignatz here. He picked me up on
        his shoulders, took a load off my
        feet.

IGNATZ *takes up the singsong.*

IGNATZ.

We ran through the jungle and came to the
        falls
The city was far below and it hadn't any
        walls
We tried to get in through the red-and-yellow
        dome
and the man from the West said: 'This won't
        get you home'
We shipped out to the Islands Behind the
        Wind
where we ate tuba fish and went stone blind
The girl in the bar sang a slow song through
        her tears
about a candle in the window. It was meant
        for us, and for two long years
We stayed there putting up phones
connecting other people's homes
In a white coin box on the sand

a bloke with a dog took the phone in hand
and shouted: 'I love you on my knees'
We'd had enough of overseas
Our ship, however, didn't go
to El Dorado. We ended up in dirty snow
We banged our spoons on our mess-tins,
shouting at every blow
We felt the stinking breath of the murderous
bear, but he let us go.
Under the angry tropic moon the war broke
out again
we were the generals, but we hadn't any men.
Beautiful were the waters, the ebbing and the
flow
and Father Anton's voice resounded from
below
Come, children, come, follow me and listen
and out of the bottomless water the
homebound runners glistened
It wasn't some nasty sawhorse he was
dragging
it was a nifty four-seater wagon.
The man with the pencil drove no-handed and
wrote on the air
I am your brother, here, there and everywhere

ANTON *takes up the singsong and carries it on.*

ANTON.

At the triple crossroads we came to a man

he was sitting under the milk stand and he
had nothing on.
He moaned and he groaned: 'Oh wretched
three roads, oh God-forsaken
gulch'
and we groaned even louder: 'Oh Rivers of
Babylon, oh Wuthering Heights, oh
Angel's Bulge'
For years we lived on bread and yellow
marmalade
in the heavens at night we saw the Symbol of
Jade
We went to the Translux Cinema and at the
first kiss we fell asleep
We flew with the black falcon to the high
plateaux, and there the snow was
deep
On Maundy Thursday, our faces reddened by
the ice-flake storm
we climbed the white bell-tower in the dawn
but instead of a clapper there were only
strands of hay
that swung in the breeze and whispered 'Oy
vay'
After that things got worse and worse and
worse
the bile-green Northern Lights brought on the
curse
Through the back door we looked, but curious

there was nobody there, not even us.
We lost our face guards, our lips stuck to the
 cold
iron pipes and no one, oh no one could break
 their hold
not even the Noble Lady in the choir
her singing fluttered like moth wings in my ear
The man with the lance wound stood eating a
 banana
around his neck like a halter a torn liana
He preached a sermon that nobody
 understood
And finally the concrete mixer settled his hash
 for good
Alas, we never saw the city's better side
never suspected what expanses the pagodas of
 terror hide
The loveliest roses smelled of watered wine
we postponed our homeward journey till some
 other time
And then (*he turns towards* THE
 CARETAKER) the girl from the
 motorway intersection appeared in
 a yellow sou'wester
on which was written Here I am, your sister
And the guide rail transmitted her personal blues
called 'I am the heart's-ease flower you can't
 refuse'
We took the tram from the Northern Star

and saw the warm-brown peat fields from afar
the house of the rising sun towered above the
trees,
and we heard the voice of the Bog Man
saying:
'We can't all do what we please – but we can
all say what we please'

The others repeat:

'We can't all do what we please – but we can
all say what we please'

THE CARETAKER *takes up the singsong and transforms it into a kind of hymn, in which the others join.*

THE CARETAKER.

Far, far from home
it will take me seven years or more
to become a native
I won't get impatient counting
but with relief
walking back and forth, myself a number
I shall return to my country.
He who in pain
bellows the world to pieces
will get an answer from the river
Sleepwalking, I shall get there
Thunderless sheet lightning
will show me my maize field
rustling valley-wide

standing, stalk after stalk
and vanishing again in the darkness
I shall walk the 'old road'
the road without cars
where the lightning-cleft bastard tree grows
The day will never come
it is already here
On the threshold of the village I shall stop
and listen
breathless, I shall expand to my people
soundlessly the sheet lightning will show me
my white walls
as they stand there
vanish
and afterglow in the darkness
Long have I been where
supposedly no one has ever been
The centre of the village will be windless
the air still warm from the heat of the day
No assembly rock will await me, but only
the cherry tree plastered with ten years of
movie posters
Under the rustling leaves
I shall be everywhere on earth
Who says that earthly magnitudes
are incompatible with celestial longitudes?
In the darkness the holiday man will greet me
as matter-of-factly as you please
and say: 'A thousand years are as a day'

but I shall resist temptation
and continue on to the next village
My kind of heart wound is soothed by a
dressing of tree leaves at eye-level
Sheet lightning changes to storm lightning
followed by thunder
but just as the first drops fall I shall come to
the yellow inn
The blond waitress will lead me from misery
along the dark arcaded shore
to brightly lit rooms of consolation
and we shall tremble with heads like flowers
and twinkle with animal eyes:
The discoverer turns womb
and the womb turns discoverer!

ALL.

When will the man with the book restore my
right?
When shall I be capable of wishing
instead of wanting to win?
For Victoria is only a *name*.
When will the city lights cease to be frosty
commercial glitter
and become signals from neighbour to
neighbour?
For Victoria is only a *name*!
When will the singer with the happy voice stop
the floods of rain

and banish the haemorrhage of guilt and
damnation
to prehistoric times from the hearts of men?
When will the episodic bell resound eternally
and when will there be one mankind
throughout the earth?
When will my frozen heart melt with feeling
and when at last shall I, shall we all, stand on
my gold ground?
For Victoria is *more* than a name!

ANTON, IGNATZ *and* THE CARETAKER *turn away and stride solemnly across the platform to the shack, which remains dark and still.* HANS *and* GREGOR *stand in the foreground, looking at the billowing construction-site curtain.*

GREGOR. Then the festival is over?

HANS. The festival prevails.

GREGOR. There are things we should talk about.

HANS. Come to the next building site. It won't be on the shady side like this one, it's on the southern slope and the valley isn't as windy. But first come home – they keep asking for you, they say you've deserted your people. That's where the festival will be, and everybody (*he gestures towards the shack*) will be there. We, the living, as well as our dead; it will be the festival of decision.

GREGOR. I watched you at work this afternoon. You were almost always alone. Every so often the foreman would come and send you somewhere else, to the grinding mill, the drier, the hammer mill. You were busy with your work, you just grinned – but then you'd look around, as though for help. From a distance you looked like an old man.

HANS. I'm what they call the handyman here. All day long they send me from one machine to another; I'm the handyman because they can use me for any job and I'm strong enough to do most jobs on my own. The handyman isn't a member of the team. From morning to night they send him up and down, back and forth, from hot to cold, from one machine to another. Have you noticed? We use hardly any tools nowadays, just machines. This is a big construction job, the next will be even bigger. They used to call us the carpentry gang, because in this work a man can't do much by himself – for most jobs several are needed. What I'm doing now is just as hard, but no skill is involved. I like working, not working drives me crazy, I get fidgety and irresponsible; but once a day I'd like to disappear into the clay, to bury my face in the clay, to be clay, to be clay in clay. At such times you can see me sitting in the movable aluminium toilet with my head between my knees, overstaying the longest cigarette break, all ready to be moved away myself. Somebody has to be the handyman, and it may as well be me. Actually the lot of us here (*he gestures towards the shack*) are just handymen. Next week we'll be moving to construction site Number Twenty. There won't be any problems to solve, we know all we need to know, and we're not learning anything new. I often long to learn something new. When I look at our finished buildings in the valleys, I see that something is lacking – a certain curvature there used to be in the roof, not some superficial ornament, but maybe a subtle line above the ribs. I'm not at all ashamed of these new buildings, actually I'm rather proud of having helped to put them up, but there's always some little detail missing that would have made them complete. The curvature is missing, the art is missing. For centuries we builders were slaves. Then for a short while we were promoted to the rank of 'workers'. Now we're slaves again – all of us, even the architects, even the geologists who tested the terrain, even the ministers who will soon dedicate the building. None of us is doing work that's worthy of a human being. Many a time at home, when everyone else is asleep at night, I sit in the dark, thinking of our dead parents, and then I wish I could be a little different. Oh yes! (*He points to his wedding ring.*) Believe me, if I had had to live all these years without a wife, I'd be dead by now. I'm not sure whether it's a great love, but sometimes when I'm near her, I feel reverence. Yes, reverence. I the prole, the commuter, the handyman, worship her, the gracious lady, who soothes and consoles me. (*He rubs the ring till it sparkles.*) And our child is my only joy. I want you to know how lonely I am. I have no one to turn to, not even myself. I am forlorn, forsaken. Don't go yet. Stay the night. There's someone I can't hear or see in the next room. He is not quiet, it's just that he doesn't make any sound, all he does is watch me. He doesn't dream, he's empty. He's weak, cold, evil. Silent, watchful, weak, cold, evil. Sometimes the emptiness here is evil. (*He gestures to indicate his surroundings.*) Don't leave me alone.

GREGOR. Is it really *me* you're talking to?

HANS. It's *you*.

3

SOPHIE *in front of the curtain.* GREGOR *joins her.*

SOPHIE. Do you know that I used to be in love with you? I wasn't just fond of you as a brother. When you came near me, I got excited, as if you were the only one. You were the man I longed for, the man I trusted. In those days I imitated your handwriting, I even copied your drawings. Whenever you came home from a trip, you behaved like a family tyrant. The others were afraid of you. I alone ignored your domineering moods, I understood them, and you were grateful to me for that. When I began to go out with boys, I was ashamed in front of you, I spoke of them as foolish children. Remember how, when our parents were away, you'd play 'head of the family', responsible for the rest of us? Later on I had the feeling that you wanted me to be for ever as calm and passionless and contented as a dear little sister should be, busy for ever and ever with dear little nothings. And so I kept my wishes, my aims, secret from you. I felt I was being unfaithful to you, and it was then that I stopped being in love with you. Your image no longer trembles inside me, the sight of you no longer warms my eyes. Because now I have an aim. It's a life dream, and that kind of dream is worth something. People who talk about the virtues of self-sacrifice are just making excuses. Anyone who makes a dream come true will be helping a lot of other people. So take your sister seriously, help her to make a place for herself. I'm entitled to it. Even the tiniest shop would be a centre and shed a friendly light – why wouldn't it shed a friendly light for you too someday? Believe me, it's a fine thing to come into a room with the feeling that you are your own master. And weren't you always saying to your brother and sister: 'There's no decision in your lives'?

GREGOR. What kind of businesswoman will you be? I can see you in mask and costume. I can hear the clickety-click of your heels when you diagnose whoever comes through the door as a customer. There will be a false glitter in your eyes, a false lilt in your voice, a false elegance in your hips, a false dance in your legs – you'll be false from top to toe. Once when I passed your place of work, I saw you in your stocking feet, squatting in the shop window with pins between your lips. There, I thought, is someone like me. No artificial energy; your movements were slow, casual, as though you were doing your work not for some boss but for me, the passer-by. You brought fresh air into that shop window. At home later on you were really at home, at the cinema you were really at the cinema, in the fields in the fields; your Sunday was a Sunday. In your stocking feet you were flesh of my flesh, you were human, something you won't be any more when you paint your face like a model. Your strikingly upright gait won't be a dance of freedom, it will be the product of a crash course. In the salesroom up front mealy-mouthed flattery will set the tone; in the workshops at the back the atmosphere will be that of the drill ground. You will have all sorts of things to sell, but you yourself will have no liking for anything. You won't see, you'll only be capable of appraising, and yet you won't be able to distinguish between men and women, children and grown-ups, the good and the expensive. But you'll be able to tell at a glance whether a pistol is loaded or not. Your emblem will be a jangling bunch of keys hanging from your cold business fingers.

Wherever you go, in the woods or at the seashore, you will hear only one sound, the rat-tat-tat of the cash register. Your home will be the chamber of commerce, and in your lifetime as on your tombstone 'shop owner' will be part of your name. Never again will there be a ring of sweat around your armpits, never again will you blush or shut yourself up in the toilet to read a letter. Once your shop sign goes up, you'll be done for, the only part of you that will fly will be your artificial hairdo. Why should you want to swell the evil legion of the living dead, why should you want to become an unperson? Why should you want to be a passing cloud of perfume, stink of decay for a little while, and then be nothing more?

SOPHIE. You're unjust. And you're ungrateful too. Have you forgotten the times when you've stepped from the street into a shop, from cold to warm, from noise to quiet, from wet to dry, from your solitary darkness into public light, from your tremulous private instant into centuries-old tranquillity, from the menacing void into a safe place, from silent harassment to the soothing ritual of buying and selling? Haven't you felt sheltered in the changing rooms, haven't they given you a chance to remake your image? Have you forgotten the beautiful woman in the background with the smooth, resplendent forehead, who sat on a stool waiting, but not for a customer? And wasn't it the owner who tossed his child into the air in the storeroom, shouting: 'I love you!'? What makes you so sure I won't be human if I stop being dependent? That's right. You've always thought the real human beings were the ones who suffered in silence. But don't you remember the evenings when I'd come home from work and roam around the garden in tears, wishing I was dead? Don't you remember that you swore to save me from that hell? Have you forgotten my pathetically soft answers to the bellowing bosses and supervisors, the terror in my eyes when it came time for the evening accounts? Have you forgotten the way the boss's son would press me against the wall? The lives of my kind of people are always inhuman, not because we have to serve others, but because it's not the right kind of service. You think it's your duty to sing our praises. But I know you: you're not a sentimentalist. You see through things and people. When you were little, the whole family was afraid of the cold, penetrating look in your eyes. And not just the family, the whole village. People complained to our parents about the way you looked at them as you passed. You're far from blind to other people. You see their misery at a glance. Your problem is that you feel as if other people's misery were your own. And since you can't overcome it and can't drop dead because of it, the only way you can save yourself is by glorifying our misery and convincing yourself that we are saved. You see clearly, and at the same time you have the power to glorify. Yes, you're not weak enough to make light of our misery, but you're strong enough to glorify it. As our proverb says, you have good will enough to pretend. But that's not enough. You're also a helper. Time and again you've come to someone's assistance. It came so natural to you that you kept out of sight. Yes, most of the time you'd hesitate for a second – but once you'd made up your mind, you were free, weren't you? So don't hesitate now. You're capable of helping and that's what gives you the right to exist. But many a time you froze. All that was asked of you was to hold out your hand, but you didn't move and that made you guilty. And the next time it was guilt that made you freeze up. The truth is you were born to be a helper. It's only as a helper that you are fully real. If you miss your chance now, you won't be able to glorify anyone any more. Your best work will cease to be work, your life will be without joy, you'll be a dragon. Believe me, I won't leave you in peace. You will be a helper, or you won't be anything at all. Whatever you do will be unreal and I will be your shadowy sister. (*She goes out to one side.*)

GREGOR (*alone in front of the curtain*). O river in the mist. O autumn colours on the far shore, which used to tell me not to be afraid. O distant ocean. O frozen will. O prehistoric rock. O dawning light, with raindrops on the dusty road, where long ago I walked with someone and was close to life. O earth, which was once called the realm of light. O summer and winter, parks and squares, tympanums and wooden benches, arbours and railway stations, woodsmoke and night flights, silence and rumbling. O river that I often answered, river to whose glitter and murmur the response time and again was 'I'! Alas, wide world! – and everywhere, amidst the clatter, the rattling, the swarming, the wriggling, the clicking, the whispering, the jostling, the speeding, the scribbling, the sweating, the pushing and shoving, the bowing and scraping, the double-talk and triple-talk of business, the hypocrisy, the treachery, the evil dissension of business, the everlasting outrage of business, the damnation of business! I will carry my case to justice. (*He starts slowly to go out on the other side, but he stops on the way and says:*) I've had a dream. I saw the property set free with the blue sky over it, and I thought. I've saved a piece of land. I've saved a piece of sky.

4

Second set. Deserted square outside the wall of a village church. The churchyard gate is open. Through it no tombstones can be seen, only luminous green. The tops of two dark thin trees, spruces or cypresses, can be seen behind the wall. To one side of the gate, outside the wall, a stone bench with a small but noticeable hollow. The lighting is bright throughout the scene. It is the light of a subdued holiday, such as All Saints, but at no particular time of year. A bell is ringing. (It sounds something like a giant guitar, resounding over the whole countryside.) An OLD WOMAN *in a plain dark holiday dress approaches through the gate; she keeps turning back as she walks, and stops front stage. She looks and listens. The bell dies away.*

THE OLD WOMAN. Must I again go away from here, the only place far and wide that I love? The border is up there, just after the crossroads, and after the border there's nothing. After the bridge the road divides into three. The first fork leads upstream to the gully where the mills used to be. Only the roofless walls are left now and the flowers that grow in the chinks aren't flowers any more. At the beginning of the gully there are still bright red raspberries, but farther on it's dark and damp, the bushes are bare, and what raspberries there are never get ripe, or they have white worms hanging from them. The last flood carried away some of the footbridges and no one will ever rebuild them. But that may be a place to hide when the next war comes; there are still a few edible mushrooms, the water is clean, you can find flints in the brook, there are some huts tucked away in the woods, and it's sunny and quiet under some of the overhanging cliffs. The second fork used to go downstream through the fields. The land is still cultivated, but there are no more smallholdings, just one big field where they grow cattle feed; that's not called maize any more, it gets its name from the towers where it's fermented. It grows so tall that you can't see the village behind it except in the wintertime. Yet sometimes this silage stuff smells as good as the old-fashioned maize, and the soft leaves bend backwards and topple over in self-abandonment as I did when I was young, not nearly often enough! And hidden behind the leaves the ears with their golden ringlets shine through their envelopes and bandages: Lazarus, rise up – Lazarus, show yourself – Lazarus, come to me. The third fork leads to the village. Where once there were puddles of spilt milk you'll now see shimmering spots of oil in the tar, and of all the sounds you'll hear there, the friendliest is the ringing of bicycle bells. If you see someone walking there at night, by the roadside that isn't a roadside, it's me. But where is the village? At the centre, they've put up a sign, saying: 'Village centre'. And the old paths are signposted too, they've been named after the rich city people who have their country houses there and pay most of the taxes. There's nothing left of the township but the town hall, which has the same plate-glass windows as the savings bank next door. Every year they sign up for a 'best-kept village' contest, the committee members water the flower beds, clip the hedges, polish the flagpoles, and give me dirty looks because my petticoat shows. Sometimes after midnight the flow of water can be heard, then apples fall on to the grass, a swarm of leaves darkens the whiteness of a headlight beam, the stars shine in the sky, and when I look up I see the Milky Way. The noise outside my window isn't a marauder, it's my night-time visitor clattering in the food dish I've put out for him. But of course that kind of friend isn't enough; all alone as I am, with everything dead all around me, I'm afraid. In the village the mopeds, at home the flies. I get shooting pains in my limbs, they climb up into my head and drive me crazy. People say I have nothing to complain about, my room is heated and I get enough to eat. My answer to that is: I'm not complaining, I'm lamenting. Every time I go from here to the junction of the three roads I feel like lying down in the grass triangle there, it's as though that were my only refuge apart from this gate. In my last hour I'd like to be taken there and disappear in the tall grass, like the blind king in the fairy tale. Maybe the village never existed. When I was a child at school, they made me kneel on a log all one morning. It broke my heart. Years later, a man proposed to me. I was scared to death, I thought it would get me with child and I'd die. 'Let's get married,' he said. 'All right,' I mumbled. After that it was never mentioned again. How strange everything here has become, I don't know if it's since the last earthquake or the last war, or since that time I had to kneel on the log. What a worthless place this village is. The church has been renovated in white and gold. How I'd love to hear the words of my God day after day instead of always seeing yellow plastic balls flying into the air. (*As though talking to the ground.*) Will I ever again look upon a dear one and be happy? (*She straightens up.*) I would like to curse this village and its inhabitants, who have stopped listening to anything but the clanging of the electrical bowling alley, I would like to curse their mouths, which are like the slits of moneyboxes, into which people put coins but nothing ever comes out. I would like to curse their phony costumes, their plaster-white stockings, their chest straps and their hartshorn buttons, as big and full of holes as death's-heads. I would like to curse their offspring, who even as children stand there like butchers, goggling with the eyes of slaughtered cattle. (*To the audience.*) You corpses, all you need is to die visibly and unmistakeably. You're not human beings, you're the opposite, beings forgetful of being. Hell may not exist, but my curse exists!

GREGOR *and* NOVA *enter front stage.* THE OLD WOMAN *goes to one side.*

GREGOR. This is where it was. Here. This is a place apart, outside the village. I have often gone from here to the village and back, sometimes walking, as often as not running, homewards on Easter morning with the burning consecrated touchwood to light the hearth fire with at home; just as I reached the door it would fall from the holder, and I'd carry the last smoking piece across the threshold in my bare hand; or in this direction, when I was sent to have the bell rung for a member of the family who had just died. I feel an affection for this spot, which is not the village, as for no foreign place, however alluring. I am positively proud to have been born near here, and it means something to me to be in the baptismal register Just now, when I saw the walls and the treetops in the distance, I wished I was already here. I flew. Everything flew. I saw this place as the realm of forms and colours cleansed of everything homelike, everything local, everything temperamental, everything typical, everything frenzied. To me this green was the heartland of all green, and the whole area a kind of perpetual antiquity, where each individual is different but where all have *one* voice, and the name of the place was the HERE COUNTRY. When the big bell sounded, I sensed that it was being heard by people in the fields, in the ditches, on the slopes, on the rooftops, in the rooms, on the tractors, and I knew what the ringing meant. And the person standing there wasn't just 'I', it was 'I and the ringing'. Never betray that ringing, I thought. Dramas can revolve around places. Maybe those are the last dramas, the dramas of dramas. Yes, this silent graveyard is my point of departure, my culture. (*He goes over to the stone bench and indicates the hollow.*) I have always thought about this hollow. It has been here for centuries, no one knows what it was for, yet to my mind it stands for the whole village. I've been away for years, but sometimes I catch myself giving this village as my address, and when I look for it on a map, I expect for some reason to see a mark shaped like this little hollow. (NOVA *goes through the arch into the graveyard and vanishes.* THE OLD WOMAN *approaches* GREGOR, *describes large circles around him, and looks at him from all sides.*)

THE OLD WOMAN. It's him. I don't have to look for scars. He's older, but he hasn't changed. When it starts to rain, he comes out of the house with a chair, sits down under the overhanging roof, folds his arms, and watches the rain. When it storms, he runs into the woods, squats between the roots of a spruce tree, and listens to the roaring in the tree tops.

He is work-shy and work-happy. He is sorry for himself but he fights back pain. He is quietly sympathetic and loud with ridicule. He is the joy and the sorrow of his parents. He neglects to ask questions but catches up on his questioning. He is our neighbour and he is our man from overseas. (*To* GREGOR.) Welcome. Infant with the guileless look. Snotnosed brat, boy with the fat behind and the juniper whipstock, teenager with the blue bicycle, city slicker with the sunglasses and white trousers, bigshot with a pocketful of loose paper money, mourner with the bending knees, stranger with the silver-bright hazel stick, man with the soundless shoes. When at last will you stay here for good and do a little something for us? When at last will you take action against the high-sounding falsehoods of the so-called representatives of the people, of the regional programmes, of questionnaires, of so-called public welfare, of electrified fences, the evil mesh of flimflam and gabble-gabble that they throw over us to kill us, to blow out the light of our souls, to smother us? (*As though to the audience.*) Revenge! (*To* GREGOR *again.*) You belong to us. Stay here and avenge us. Drive the Tyrolean hats out of our mountains. Expose the peasant costumes as anachronistic rubbish. Button our murderers' soft-leather flies to their hard-leather war masks. Show that every one of their words is barking, show that their mouths are full of barbed wire. Make ready the winding sheets for our contemptuous listeners and make them in their last hour listen to their present laughter.

Both smile.

GREGOR. You have always expected something of somebody here. I remember my grandfather telling me about a man who went away, across the seas supposedly, and everyone thought he'd come back some day and then everything would be all right. Some of these legendary figures actually did come back and set themselves up as sages. But did any of them go on being legendary once they were here? And what of the man who lost his roots on his travels? About whom the proverb says: 'That is how all the truly great kings of life die'? It's time you stopped expecting someone to come and atone for some guilt or relieve you of some curse or tell you miraculous tales about some other place. Don't the winds of the world blow here? Aren't there days when the tiniest brooklet glitters like a faraway river? Haven't you more than once glimpsed a foreign mountain in the moonlight?

And once the weeks-long rain stops, has it been anything more than a brief shower in silent eternity? The living fire burns here too, your bread is bread, and the freshly pressed juice in your cellar is wine. The pre-war coffee tin is resplendent with an exotic dancing girl, pomegranates glow behind the withering larch, and at night the branches of your trees are magnified by Orion's golden branch. You too have been overseas. You have even been on the moon. You've been on every moon. But the lands beyond the seas and continents also have their wretched and forsaken, and there too the gibberish of false learning usurps power. And you, dear old woman, favoured with a supermarket calendar, greeted in church with stupid stupid evil tabloid headlines, bombarded in your very broom cupboard by the loudspeaker cars passing in the High Street, you too, right here, speak the language of adventure.

THE OLD WOMAN. You haven't changed. You still come out for reconciliation, the way you did in the old childhood fights. But not even you will be able to sidestep conflict now. There's a rumour going round the village that you and your brother and sister are planning to burden your parents' farm with a bank loan.

Your sister has been seen several times with a man from the bank. I'm told that they both talk uncommonly fast and the key word that keeps coming up is 'mortgage'. Your brother sat there saying nothing, and I'm told the other two talked long and fast at him too. Afterwards, he said to some other people: 'I'm only a worker, I don't know anything about business.' But there's one thing that he said over and over again: 'She's my sister after all.' And when we tell him that no good can come of it, that your sister will never be a businesswoman, that he and his family will have to move away, he says: 'One way or another I'm lost.' He also says: 'If the house goes, all this land will go. And if the land goes, it will be the end of me too.' He even said: 'And that's just what I want. I'm looking forward to war. I'm looking forward to my death. Then at last I won't have to commute any more – then there will be a different kind of travel. No more short absences. Bring on the big absence. No more Sunday outings. Bring on the forced marches. Enough of the garden. Out into the tundra. No more children's voices –the era of bellowing is back again – And after all she's my sister. And after all she's my sister!'

NOVA *comes back through the gate and joins the other two.*

NOVA. There is no one in there, but the stage seems set for an event, as if something were going to happen soon, this very day, this very hour. The chinks in the walls are ready to point guns through, as they were centuries ago, and the gilt letters on the war memorial glitter. Moths and other night creatures come fluttering from the dark inside of the box hedges. The octagonal charnelhouse is full of empty beer bottles. Transparent plastic has been thrown over the embroidered altar cloth, and a dying hornet is crawling around on it. Many of the tombstones are inscribed with a foreign language. Yet there's nothing uncanny about the place. The sky over the rectangle is like the vault over a large room. When I walked in the diagonal down below, a plane flew along the diagonal overhead. The bell swayed gently in the belfry, it looked at first like someone on a swing. Through the gate at the back you can go out into an orchard. It seems to me that this is not just a place, it's a setting, a scene, an arena, and the dark marks on the walls are not the soot of the past, but the colour of things to come, of a storm, of swarming arrows that will darken the sun. I sense the emptiness before the feast day. And at the same time the shelter of an entrenchment.

She takes GREGOR*'s arm and they go into the graveyard together.*

GREGOR (*to* THE OLD WOMAN, *before disappearing through the gate*). You won't tell anybody I'm here.

THE OLD WOMAN (*alone*). But the whole village knows. Even the neighbouring villages know. Maybe no one will explicitly recognise you, maybe no one will speak to you – but the whole valley knew long ago that you were here. Didn't the inspector in the local train punch your ticket without the least sign of recognition and then tell everyone in the next compartment that you were on your way? You heard him yourself, didn't you? And really there was nothing respectful, let alone affectionate, about the way he bellowed your name from carriage to carriage. And didn't the driver of the yellow local bus point you out to everyone who got in? And really the way he pointed his thumb at you over his shoulder didn't suggest that he was proud of you or respected you, let alone that he was glad to see you. At this very moment the word that's on everybody's lips in the village is: '*That* one is here.' You're in the wrong country, my boy. You're in a country that's small and malicious; full of prisoners who have been forgotten in their cells and even fuller of forgetful jailers, who after every outrage grow fatter in office. Their voices sound as if death-rattle amplifiers had been built into their throats, their arms and legs are like poisoned grappling irons, their eyes breed killer wasps at every glance. Not even your absence has done you any good with them. Compassion has been lost in this country. Go back home to your foreign parts. It's only there that you are *at home*, only there that joy is close to the soil. Find yourself a bigger country. A human being needs a bigger country, he needs forsakenness. And where are the forsaken here? Rest assured. Nobody loves you. And they won't leave you alone in there. Even now they are coming for you – That suits me to a T. That way I can stay here, I won't have to go back yet to the blue filling station and the black window. (*She sits down on the stone bench and puts up her hand as though to shade her eyes.*) I see something you don't see. They're coming on the run. In olden times they'd have been wrapped in a cloud of dust, the earth would have trembled under their horses' hooves, white foam would have fallen on the ground. The snorting of the horses would have been amplified by the tin visors over their nostrils, and their war song would have meant: The time has come – at last these hills, these ravines, these crops, these clearings will revert to what they were intended for: a battlefield. No more pretending; peace has never been. They have masks instead of faces, their eyes are shrunk to darkening pupils, impenetrable and dilated by sadness like the eyes of the kings of old before they set out for the realm of the dead. And his brother is in the lead, waving the black flag. From now on, the front is here.

HANS *comes in from one side holding his son by the hand.* ANTON, IGNATZ, *and* ALBIN *are his retinue. They all move rather slowly and calmly. They are wearing their dark holiday suits and hats that they take off as they approach the gate. In one hand* HANS*'s son is carrying a disproportionately large hazel stick, and in the other a small tin moneybox, which he shakes once, making the coins rattle. In advancing,* THE CHILD, *unlike the grown-ups, keeps spinning around. All stop outside the gate.*

HANS. Danger! Don't take that as a warning; danger is what I want. I'm used to danger. I need it, I'm addicted to it. If I have to spend a whole day without balancing on at least one ridgepole, I get fidgety. You fellows have seen me on the job. Where there's danger, I'm always first in line. At the edge of the highest bridge, putting up the railing, I sing with my best voice. The bloke who sits with you cowards in the gondola on the arm of the crane, laughing at your terror-stricken rabbit's eyes every time it sways, who gives it an extra little jolt to make it almost turn over – that's me. Me and nobody else. Without danger I don't exist. A single day at home in the village with my wife and child, and I start pacing back and forth like a caged tiger. The garden and the trees aren't enough for me, and racing around in a car isn't the kind of danger I mean. Some day when I've been here in this safe place from morning to night, you'll see a man running out on the road with a knife, ready to run amok. I go to the bar instead, and by midnight you'll see a man with his head on the table. At least there's that cliff with the overhanging ledge and the village down below, ten times too far to spit on; I've been there today and not alone – I had to have somebody with me, and it was him (*he points at his son*). He screamed. Did he scream! But that's not the danger I mean either. The effect doesn't last, so now I'm restless again. And not just restless. Miserable. Danger, where are you? Life-enhancing abyss, where are you? Everything is wretched, everything from here to the horizon. The pain is here (*he points*), always has been. I shall turn to my dead (*he points in the direction of the graveyard*). Haven't they, time and again, been the green grass over my heart? I talk to them in the darkness, and they appear, in the eyes of a cat, in the grazing of a branch against the windowpane in the night wind, even in the rumbling of the refrigerator. As they lie there in the earth, the skeletons are approachable. I'll sit down with them, it will do me good. They don't want anything from me and they're not angry. If I think away all my encumbrances, there they are, not my dead any more, but my saints, my saviours. I show my profile to the false abundance of the daily news, and it gives me an extra profile in empty space. (*He points.*) I stay with them here and my bad blood flows in a different way. My dead are not night ghosts – they go with the brightest part of the day, and I'm not asleep when I touch them, I'm awake. They are with me. Yes, sometimes I have a feeling that they're looking at me, in a friendly way. (*He turns towards the empty gate.*) Dear dead, smile at me again. Wink at me. Show yourselves in your light and infect me with your vitality. With your support, I'll be able again to climb stairs three at a time. Welcome me again, when I step into the abandoned house, with a note saying: There's hot food in the oven. Be a bold fresh breath to me, which will tell me at last the right thing to do. Give me again that apple with the hole in it, I'll look through the hole and see cosmic blue again. Yes, my dead, deepen the blue of the sky for me. Dance closer to me against the light, with that bend of the hips and dangling of the wrists that have never before been seen in a death dance, with the delicate rounded shoulders, the chalk-white cheeks, the glinting eyes, on country lanes, in sunlight colours that have never been seen in any representation of the dead. Do it today, do it now; make my heart stand still as it did then, which didn't mean that I wasn't alive, but set the measure for my being alive. Be my measure, like the flowing river, the shining sun, the first raindrops on the dry leaves. My dead, greetings. (*He goes through the gateway with the three others.* THE CHILD *stands there a moment, then sits down with* THE OLD WOMAN *on the stone bench, on the other side of the hollow. He leans his stick against the wall and rattles the moneybox once.*)

THE OLD WOMAN. Do you believe in miracles? (THE CHILD *shakes his head and rattles.*) When I was young, I worked in the next valley for a while. I was terribly alone there; it was as if I had only one eye, this big, and couldn't close it. There was a basket full of pumpkins in the yard. When I was sent to empty it, there were five dozen eggs on the black tar at the bottom, lying on a bunch of blue cornflowers. The pumpkins had flattened the eggs, but they weren't broken. And then I heard a voice (*she remembers*); oh, such a sweet voice, never again as long as I've lived have I heard such a sweet voice, and the voice said to me: 'See the miracle and forget it. See the miracle now and forget it right away.' (THE CHILD *nods and rattles.*) When I was back home again, my poor dead father (*she points behind her*) noticed something about me, but I had decided not to say anything. He asked me: 'Do I have to tickle your story out of you like an egg out of a hen?' So I told him the whole story. (*Remembering.*) 'Like an egg out of a hen, out of its arsehole.' (*She points and laughs.* THE CHILD *laughs too, points and rattles.* THE OLD WOMAN *thinks back and remembers her father's original sentence.*) 'Bom ščegetal zgodbo iz tebe kot jayce iz kokoši.' – Glej čudez in pozabi! See the miracle and forget. (*She laughs.* THE CHILD *rattles.* THE OLD WOMAN *remembers some more.*) Slavčeg med trnjem/se je zganil/in zapel;/bel cvet divje rože/je zakrvavel . . .' The nightingale in the bramblebush moved and began to sing; the white wild rose began to bleed . . . (THE CHILD *rattles.* THE OLD WOMAN *looks up.*) I see the last guest coming to our festival. Faceless, she comes barging in, with no eyes for the place she is coming to. (*She stands up,* THE CHILD *does likewise.*) She is a white averted cheek. In the old days I would have called out: 'The wild huntress is coming.' And thought: 'Save me!' But now I think: 'Whom can I save?' Sorrow. Grief. No miracle is possible. (*She goes out through the gate.* THE CHILD *follows her. Almost at once* SOPHIE *comes in from the side calmly and rather slowly.*)

SOPHIE. Didn't I like myself once? When fear and trembling came, didn't I look in the mirror and didn't my girlfriend in the mirror smooth me down? Alone in bed, alone in my room, alone in the cold, didn't I always curl up inside the warm cave that was me? Wasn't there a great moment at least once a day when gently, wondrously, the angel that was myself flew over me? Then I was in the light, all was well because I liked myself. Why don't I like myself any more? Is it only children that have a 'me', and is my childhood over? Since when have I been counting how often other people say 'I' as if the word should be held against them? I don't want to be wicked. But neither do I want to go back. I want a decision. I refuse to spend the rest of my days as your drudge; I'm going to assert myself with passion and make myself known as a woman of action. I'll be proud of it. Don't bother me with your house and home and your artificially lit shrines. When I came home, didn't I think as often as not: 'What am I going to do here?' Didn't I prefer any amount of waiting at dark, rainy bus stops to the smells and sounds and voices in the warm, dry, brightly lit house? Didn't I many a time, sitting at table with the family, long to be gone from there to the most disagreeable work, alone in the hindmost, draftiest corner of the storeroom? What a kerfuffle about a house. I look up at the sky and think, I've got a home in the clouds, and that's enough for me. A grooved leaf is my nine-armed chandelier. And who says that a bank is necessarily such a bad place? Can't the feel of the place be friendlier than in any wall-clock-ticking living room or fluffed-up featherbedded bedroom, where you could die for want of air to breathe? This much I know: A stranger in a bank can turn out to be somebody, while at home there's usually nobody. And as far back as I can remember, I haven't expected love from the members of my family, but only from strangers. (*She goes quickly through the gate.*)

For a moment the stage is empty. Then the three workers come out, followed by THE OLD WOMAN *and* THE CHILD. THE OLD WOMAN *and* THE CHILD *sit down again on the stone bench.* ANTON, IGNATZ, *and* ALBIN *go out to one side and come back immediately with a wooden ladder, which they set up against the outer side of the wall. One of them climbs up and looks into the graveyard. There is no sound to be heard from there. The man on the ladder turns to the others and holds his hat in front of his face. He climbs down and the next climbs up. He looks into the graveyard, turns to the others and holds his nose. He climbs down; the third wants to climb up, but the other two hold him fast.* THE CHILD *moves closer to* THE OLD WOMAN. *The three others stand at the foot of the ladder. All, including* THE CHILD, *put on their own masks.* GREGOR, HANS, *and* SOPHIE, *without* NOVA, *approach slowly through the gate and stop in the foreground; they too are wearing their own masks. They stand approximately in a triangle;* SOPHIE *and* GREGOR *at roughly the same distance from the audience, facing each other;* HANS *in the middle and further back, almost in the gateway.*

SOPHIE (*to* GREGOR). Do you remember, brother, how you once told me to hold out my hand and then you spat in it? Do you remember how later, when you came home from the city, you walked through the village with us, keeping your distance as if you had never had anything in common with us? In those days I still liked to take your arm. But you pressed your arm to your side and kept away from us. You were ashamed of your family, you denied us. What really was so remarkable about you? You were superior to your brother and me, but only because you were the one who knew how to talk. 'Yes, he can talk all right'; even our parents (*she points at the graveyard*) used to say that – not with unmixed approval, as I realise now for the first time. You claimed to feel responsible for us – but what did you ever do for us? You have no real right to the house and land, your work benefits no one but you, and all you've rightfully earned by it up to now is a chair and a table. Haven't you yourself admitted that you don't even deserve the chair you sit on, or the view out of the train window, or the blanket that covers you at night, or the bread you eat, because you've done nothing to earn them? Haven't you yourself said that the things you think you've hewn in stone sometimes fly up from the ground and blow away? That your so-called work can never be anything but hollow presumption – because the Holy Scriptures have already been written and the holy pictures have already been painted. So now stop listening to your inner voice and listen to someone else: In the eyes of the people hereabouts, a year of your labour is worth less than the uncorking of a bottle, than a turn of the crank on a coffee mill or the pressure of a ballpoint pen on the key of a cash register. People disapprove of you. I disapprove of you.

HANS (*steps forward*). War at last. The festival of festivals! Let no bunker save us. Doom is our triumph. Hear the whimper of the perishing dog. His right name is 'Long Misery'. Forget the official name. At last the word. The word is 'War'. That was the word in the beginning and so shall it be in the end. What joy to be irreconcilable for ever. Let everything perish. This child (*he points*), my flesh and blood? Water under the bridge. Let him be a member of every hostile gang. The blue mountain in the summer? (*He points.*) Water under the bridge. Never again shall a bus arrive with a familiar face in it. The three of us here, all laughing, pressing our faces together in the flash of a photo booth? Water under the bridge. Never again will the star Aldabaran come flickering out from behind the moon, the way our lighters used to flicker behind our cupped hands on draughty building sites. Let our faces imprint themselves on clay, or nowhere from this day on. Let there be nothing more in the clay, and far and wide no eyes. Let the grass grow without our colour vision. Let the river meander and seep away without the moisture of our eyes. Without our answering shimmer the rock face shimmers no more. Gate of the last world war, open up. Dog of war, bark and grab us (*gesture*), grab them all. Let eternal night throw its black sack over our heads and (*gesture*) draw the string. Supposedly beloved planet, supposedly peace-loving earth, expose yourself at last as a secret superweapon, that bellows as it revolves (*he circles round two or three times; the others move out of his way*): Colourless, humourless, abysmally stupid death, take us all, finish us off.

He starts to leave, but waits, as though what he has said may not be the last word after all.

GREGOR. A few centuries ago it was the custom in this valley to make so-called leaf masks. The leaves were carved out of wood, a mouth opened in the middle, and human eyes looked out. I once saw us – and we weren't the only ones – like that in the leaves. One autumn day I was walking in a big park, the ground was covered with fallen leaves and glowed with the reflection of the sunset sky. Now and then the leaves moved, a leaf would jump up or turn a somersault. And as I was walking along, our faces and stories rose up from the leaves. They were *one* face and *one* story, and that one face and one story, as I've discovered since, must be the aim of work, not only my work, but the work of us all. The motion of those fallen leaves in the grass was the gentlest anyone has ever seen. But now it's as though we were all separate individuals running away in the dark, crunching and crackling like the footfalls of dogs or hunters. Here is my decision: The two of you, consider the house and land as yours, and do what you like with them. I waive my claim, and it doesn't even hurt very much. At the moment I feel almost relieved. Gamble the land away if you like –

Why not? The likes of us have no business owning land or a house, it's only as losers that we can be ourselves. We are descended from losers, who rolled into their graves like cheeses (*gesture*), and we will roll after them in the same way, each in turn. Perhaps we shall somehow meet now and then after this, but we shall never see one another again. Yes, we are seeing one another now for the last time. (*He turns abruptly to the child.*) And here he sits, the future loser, the next instalment of our story. Here he sits on his white, loser's arse, which soon enough a multitude of game tenants (*indicates the surrounding country*) will pepper with birdshot. Already he has the stupid look of a man condemned in advance. He has nothing to be proud of but the explosive pop of his bubblegum. (THE CHILD *rattles softly.*) He'll be a slave like his father and grandfather, and he'll have no qualms about begetting yet another slave, who in turn will beget a new generation of slaves. Never will he father the thought of any heritage worth handing down. Devoid of memory or orientation, he and his like will crawl into any old hole in the ground, and only in war games look up in any particular direction. He will be one of those loudmouths who speak in the name of all, and whom nobody wants. He will jingle coins in places where there is nothing for him to buy, and talk big while those who have the say despise him in silence. One of these days little things will be missing from other children's schoolbags, and he will be the snickering thief. He will be the intrepid fireman, and he will be the firebug. A dead body will be found in the maize field, and he will be the murderer. Or he will be none of all these, but the friendliest of men, smoothing over every quarrel with his gentleness. And one day he will hang his head and say with a long drawn-out, never-ending moan: 'The village of' – you supply the name – 'revolts me. I am worthless. All humans are worthless.' And once again a man will be lost. And the game tenants will nod and say: 'Too bad.' And I, I will not be your stand-by any more. Now I know that you, my brother and sister, are the evil ones. (THE CHILD *rattles to chase away* GREGOR'*s words.*)

SOPHIE. You have no right to say such things. Go away. For good.

GREGOR. It hurt me to say such things.

SOPHIE. It hurts me to say that this is no longer the place for you.

GREGOR. We have all forfeited this place.

SOPHIE. No one from the same village, the same valley, talks like you. Only the evil one.

GREGOR. The evil one who is choked with tears? The evil one with the heavy arms? The evil one with the pain here? (*He points to his heart.*)

NOVA *steps into the gateway from behind and stands there without a mask.*

SOPHIE. The pain is here in me and it says to you: You are falling. You are on your way down. And you are alone in your fall. No ray of hope is possible for someone like you, who destroys another person's delight in his own being, who does the wickedest thing in the world, stealing a child's future in the name of an insane idea. (*They turn away from each other and towards the audience.*)

GREGOR. Terrible misunderstanding.

SOPHIE. Rid us of your presence, let us live in peace.

HANS (*softly to his three friends*). Say 'Woe.'

THE THREE (*softly*). Woe.

HANS (*softly*). Who will help?

THE THREE. Who will help?

HANS. Look away from me.

ANTON. The river has gone dry.

IGNATZ. The milk stand has been torn loose.

ALBIN. The village tavern is out of wine.

HANS. It is hard to walk on the earth.

ANTON. The sun is made of ice.

IGNATZ. It refuses to shine.

ALBIN. Behind the evil moon I see another more evil one rising.

HANS. O stars, look down at last on other inhabitants of the earth.

ANTON. The man at the well is a good-for-nothing.

IGNATZ. The barefooted lady doesn't pick up the hem of her skirt in the grass any more.

ALBIN. The boy with the red waistcoat is spitting on us.

HANS. The girl pulling up the bucket at the well is no longer a picture of life. Sing the lament. Sing in time. Rise up against so-called Creation and sing, sing out of tune at the top of your voices, our song of lamentation and revenge!

They sing out of tune at the top of their voices.

ANTON. Vanished the shores of love.

IGNATZ. I lie shivering on no beach.

ALBIN. My brain is writhing in a broken nutshell, no man with the password helps me out, never again will anyone sit tenderly down beside me. My despairing gaze finds no pair of eyes, my lips twitch with bewilderment, and I gasp to no heaven in the last waves before the nothing-nothing-nothing.

HANS (*turns to* THE OLD WOMAN). There is no consolation.

THE OLD WOMAN. There is no consolation.

HANS. There is neither insight nor certainty. There is no whole, and what I think I think alone, the thought that comes to me alone is not truth but opinion, there is no such thing as universal reason, and a common goal of mankind is more than ever a will-o'-the-wisp.

THE OLD WOMAN. There is no vinegar left in the mother of vinegar.

HANS. The millstones rumble in the man with the saviour's face.

THE OLD WOMAN. No child, no saved soul, rises from the mouths of the dying.

HANS. The church spires are a forest of spears in enemy country.

THE OLD WOMAN. The wounded flank stinks and the glittering ruby-red stars belong to the murderous bear.

HANS (*turns to* THE CHILD). There is no unity between above and below. (THE CHILD *rattles.*) The blue of the sky is only the childish blue of our prayers. (THE CHILD *rattles.*) No one wants us and no one ever wanted us. (THE CHILD *rattles. Little by little, all the others except* NOVA *join in* HANS*'s chant.*) Our houses are trellises of despair built in empty space. (THE CHILD *rattles.*) Our winding staircases, whether turning to the left or right, lead to nothing but piles of old newspapers. (THE CHILD *rattles.*) If the stone heralds with the boughs of peace on the cornices of our palaces are mute, it is not only because of the roaring machines, and if they are black it is not only because of exhaust fumes (THE CHILD *rattles*); little by little they are ceasing to be stone statues (THE CHILD *rattles*), they are blowing away like sand. We're not on the wrong road, we're on no road at all. We're not rooted, we're congealed. Sailing on the high seas, we are stopped, bound, gagged, artificially respirated by the air of nowhere, in a soundproofed wall cupboard, where only evil is real and we cannot even, as the old proverbs said, appeal to our own heart. Yes, a dead weight drags me down, bends my body into a death ship, and the worst of it is that instead of blessing the living as the dying used to do, we even spoil their feast days. For who among us, in going under, utters the name of a loved one? (*He suddenly bursts out laughing.*) But now at least our own depravity, and that goes for all of us, shakes me with uncontrollable mirth. (*He spins about in a grotesque dance, then stops and wails:*) How forsaken is mankind. How forsaken is mankind.

NOVA *joins the group and the others gradually turn towards her, last of all* HANS. *She makes a sign to* ANTON, IGNATZ, *and* ALBIN, *then disappears through the gate. The three then carry the ladder, which has been leaning against the outer wall, through the gate into the graveyard and come back again.* NOVA*'s torso then appears above the wall, upon which she leans.* THE CHILD *takes the stick and slams it down with the help of* THE OLD WOMAN. *All turn towards* NOVA. *She speaks calmly, easily, but with a note of urgency. At times she has great difficulty in speaking.*

NOVA. It's only me, someone from another

village, not very different from this one. But believe me: the spirit of the new age speaks in me, and this is what it has to say to you: Yes, there is danger, and it is only because of the danger that I can speak as I am going to – words of resistance. Hear, then, my Dramatic Poem – You will do well to stop dreaming the livelong day, but don't wake one another by barking like dogs. You're not barbarians, and none of you is guilty. Your outbursts of despair may have shown you that you are not in despair at all. If you despaired, you would be dead. You can't give up. This is no time to play lonely. If you preserve some feeling for yourselves, you will see in your forsakenness a shimmer of the gods. Gods. Yes, the word exists, and no other can replace it. It's true that your whole history doesn't offer a single consolation that holds water. But stop breaking your heads about being and non-being; being is and can be thought about, whereas non-being is unthinkable, the most you can do is brood about it. You should know how equal you are – and in what ways you are equal. Who is telling you all this? I and no one else. But that can be more than it seems. 'I' can be the lightest and gentlest thing under the sun, but it can also be all-embracing, disarming. 'I' is the only hero – and you shall be the disarmers. Yes, 'I' is the human nature that preserves mankind. War is far from here. Let what has happened between you be your last conflict, let what has just been said be unsaid. *Our* armies are not grey-in-grey on concrete emplacements but yellow-in-yellow amidst yellow blossoms, and the flower stands exalted, our secret king. Yes, it is possible to bow down to a flower. The bird in the branches can be spoken to, and there is meaning in its flight. Therefore, in a world wrecked by artificial colours, work patiently for nature's regenerative colours. Mountain-blue *is* – gun-holster brown is *not*, and whoever and whatever is known to you through television is *not* known to you. Go out into the free untrammeled plain, see colours near you, see forms in the distance, radiant colours at your feet, and cloud forms overhead. Forms and colours, they are your protectors. Our shoulders are made for the sky, and between earth and sky we are the only link. Walk slowly and you yourself will become the form without which nothing can take shape in the distance; without contours you will not be their masters. Distrust superlatives, they are a matter of mood – highest peaks cannot be conquered, they can only be enjoyed – slowly. Enter into the moment of the rising sun, it will be your measure – just the sun and you. The sun will beckon you on, it will help you. The one thing I can promise you is *nature* – the only reliable promise. In nature nothing is ever finished as in the world of games, where it must then be asked: 'And what now?' True, nature can neither be a refuge nor an escape. It provides a model and a measure; but the measure must be taken each day anew. The yellow butterfly gives warmth to the blue of the sky. A tree top is the true weapon of liberation. (*She points.*) Convince yourselves – follow the bulletless line of flight – look up. Watch the drifting clouds. When they start racing, slow down. When my innermost heart trembles with the trembling of the river in the distance, then and only then do I exist. (THE CHILD *slams the stick down. The caravan music begins.*) Who says that failure is inevitable? Don't listen to the gasps of the dying: they lie. Think it over. Your war is behind you, isn't it? So shore up the peaceful present and show the calm of survivors. The 'I' is calm. And the knowledge that you are survivors will keep you warm too. What we have here is the opposite of a hospital, and what from a distance may have looked like the menacing head of death turns out, when we come closer, to be a child's game. The black eye-sockets belong to a friendly old man. Shake up your thousand-year bed. Bestir yourselves. A bedridden life is not for you. Your art is for the healthy, artists are those who are capable of living – they mould us all. Ignore the doubters who were never children. Keep your eyes open. Don't wait for another war. The wisest people are those who live face to face with nature. Look at the country and evil stupidity will pass. Haven't you all known the faraway? The faraway exists somewhere – without a house, without a second residence. Stop your double-talk, don't show yourself to your offspring with the devil's profile. Your tower of strength is the face of your fellow man. And despise frivolous mockery: reality still exists; be grateful. Gratitude is enthusiasm, and only what is thanked for lasts – gratitude can open up the wide world to you. The feast of gratitude is here and now. Peace offers an opportunity for work. Don't let it be said of you that you failed to take advantage of it. But make sure that your work is effective, pass something on. But to pass something on, one must love. Love one thing, that is enough. Only love can enable you to see things as they are. You alone, my Beloved, are real. Loving you, I awaken to myself. (THE CHILD *slams down the stick,*

THE OLD WOMAN *beside him helps him.*) And now that you have managed at last to be serious, don't cheapen your seriousness with jokes. There's no such thing as a good joke. A lot of people, however festively they may dress, are incapable of seeing with a festive eye. Most people are incapable of regeneration. Be the exceptions. Yes, there aren't many of you. But a few can count for a great deal. Ignore the schemers, the two-footed beasts. They may be sly, but you are real. Follow the caravan music. Mankind as a whole is dauntless. (*She climbs a rung higher.*) Keep going until you can make out details, until you can distinguish perspective amidst the confusion, so slowly that the world belongs to you again, so slowly that it becomes clear in what sense it does *not* belong to you. Steer clear of the impotent power that calls itself power. The good power is the power to overlook. Destroy – but only with light. Move – for then you can be slow. Slowness is the secret, and sometimes the earth is very light: a hovering, a drifting, a weightless image, a realm of reason, a producer of light. Take that image with you for your further journey; it will show you the way, and without an image of the way you will not be able to *think* any further. Don't complain of being alone – be even more alone. Hardship provides a home. Back there in the pitch darkness a pond is shimmering; back there beyond the tombstones, the pyramids are shimmering; just outside, a tree whishes by, it is a bus. Hand down that whishing. Communicate the horizon. Use the power of beautiful communication – stop the beautiful from having once again been nothing. Impart life's images to one another. What was good shall be. Slow down with the help of colours – and invent. See the green, hear the ringing of the bells, transform your involuntary sighs into powerful songs. In authentic moments you will naturally send up a cry to the gods. A cry to the gods is form and form reveals the arcade in space; our art must aim at crying out to the gods! Listen to the singing of the creators. There is a countryside you will be able to turn around in, the emptiness behind you will again be fruitful, the emptiness ahead of you will be filled with the expectations of walkers to come and the cold satellite will again be 'the keen-sighted moon'. Behold the fruitful countryside, and don't let anyone talk you out of beauty. Overwhelming is the beauty created by us human beings. Keep inventing new riddles. Busy yourselves with the unriddling that will throw light on the One Riddle, the riddle that you and I are when we wake up in the morning and go to bed at night. Haven't you all spent many nights without fear, forehead to forehead with a child, an animal, or just the empty air, and haven't you rediscovered yourselves with the shapes of the constellations? Gratitude is two friendly eyes, the opposite of the two daggers in them. Remember this: whenever a child stares at you, you are the cause. (*She climbs a rung higher. The music becomes increasingly distinct and urgent up to the end.*) On your further path you are fated to take many disguises and, rightly, you will prefer many a light-hearted hoax to every official truth. There is strength in acting as if. Yes, deny yourselves, conceal yourselves, you who are, say you are not. Only the reticent remember. Don't scruple to act out the farces of daily life – the sentences, gestures, glances. You can't always be in possession of yourselves – losing yourself is part of the game. Play your game – but let it be inspired. Yet only the unmasked can walk proudly! (THE CHILD *slams the stick down.*) Many a time your role will be that of the living dead. Shut your eyes and brighten your lost face. Shut your eyes and the after-image of the sun will bring forth a new continent. Go out into the unknown continent, with human slowness. I see ahead of us a vast realm that is still empty. Let those who are without illusions sneer. Illusion is vision, and vision is true. (THE CHILD *slams his stick down; all remove their masks.*) On your way, don't disregard the thresholds between one domain and the next. Your knowledge of transitions will bring the wind of the next domain. The circling ravens are not birds of evil omen, they are bringing food to you heroes. Yes, imbued with form and yearning, communicate the intact world – derisive laughter about it is mindless. Such laughter is misnamed; it is the death rattle of moribund souls. Mephisto is not the central character. The voice of contradiction has run out of juice. The tempters are in a different play, and if death frightens you, you've got it wrong. The dead are additional light – they transform you. Don't let it trouble you that you can't talk to them; a syllable is enough. But more important, think of our unborn, curled up in the womb – transform yourselves. Engender the child of peace. Yes, raise up the children of peace, save your heroes. Let them say compellingly: War, leave us alone. (*She climbs one or two rungs higher, until she is almost standing on the wall.*) You people of this village. It's you who count. There's nothing sinister, nothing monstrous about you. You are mysterious and inexhaustible. Don't let anyone tell you that we are sterile and unviable, the products of a late or final period. Don't listen to talk about those born too late. We are inferior to no one. We are as close to the source as ever, and each one of us is destined to conquer worlds. Shall our lifetime not be a triumphant episode? Yes, our lifetime shall be a triumphant episode. Maybe there are no wildernesses left; but there is still *a* wilderness, forever new. That wilderness is time. There is always something important going on. The tinny ticking of the clock means nothing. Time is the vibration that helps you through the accursed century, and it is also the luminous tent of survival. Only the unseeing take that as an image. Time, I have you. People of this village: forget your longing for the holy places and years of the past. The holy wide world is with you. The holy day is now. Working effectively, you can see it and feel it. Now means colours. You are now, and you are the ones who count. Your existence is a fact. Act accordingly. Stop mulling over the existence or non-existence of God. The former makes you dizzy, the latter kills the imagination, and without imagination no matter can take on form. Form is the god who is valid for all. The perception and imprinting of form heals matter. Godless and alone, we waver. Perhaps there is no such thing as rational belief, but there *is* a rational belief in divine wonderment. Divine intervention exists and you have all known it. It occurs at the moment when menacing black becomes the colour of love, the moment when you are able to say and proclaim: I am the world. You weep and the world weeps, you laugh and the world laughs. If we raise our eyes slowly, the faces of the gods smile at us out of the things of this world. – See the miracle and forget it – And the voice of the godhead says: You can love yourself. Better for you to be dead if you cannot love yourselves. People of this moment, get close to one another, discover one another as gods. Endurers of space, preservers of space. Wish, become, be, don't carry on like dogs, the sight of which demolishes the imagination. Human beings, gods fled from the gods. Take the big leap. Be the gods of change. Everything else leads to nothing – Nothing else leads anywhere now. Joy is made possible by helpfulness to friends, and friendship dances round the world. Joy is the one legitimate power. It builds a transparent tower into the landscape – an everyday, reliable tower, asking only to be climbed. With the breath of joy the submerged island rises up from the regulated river. Only joy can make things right. (*She speaks more and more slowly.* THE CHILD *slams the stick down.*) People of this moment. People of joy: It is true, still true that our whole history offers no consolation that holds water. Who can pass judgment? The mighty child-murderers go down to darkness unpunished, and the murdered souls – are our souls not our children? – remain unavenged. Tranquillity is episodic: only the eternally driven are alive. What a moment ago was the first tree of a grove dissolves into nothingness at our next glance, and the flowing fountains turn to barricades. Hope is the wrong heartbeat. We cannot, as we pass, ignore those desolate moans. Killjoys are everywhere; from no life, even the most successful, are they absent. The sorrow of sorrows makes us turn off from the beautiful river which flows from primeval to primeval, and await with uncomprehending horror the grotesquely rapid plunge into death. No, we cannot want to be nothing. Walking beneath the sun of joy, we taste bitterness deep within us. Dear people of this village, nowhere in our human history is there a consolation that holds water. The cries of horror will go on for ever. Our shelter is nowhere. The only effective way of praying is to give thanks; your pleas for mercy are engulfed by emptiness.

Don't expect the supernatural. But doesn't it console you to see a leaf float slowly down the stream? After a moment of blind grief a moment of humour. So pull yourselves together. See the man in the dark suit and white shirt, see the woman across the river, sunning herself on the balcony. Demonstrate, with the means at your disposal, your human defiance of the all-devourer. A person who is alive will find other life. Blessed be every kiss, however brief. And now, back to your places, all of you. Move with unconscious slowness. Follow the glittering lines of these boards, follow them into space. Advancing slowly, form an endless ring. Breathe spirit into space by repetition. Calm with determination, the world emerges. Only a community of creators, each in his place, can grow and be joyful like children. Your bed is in the open. Make your way through emptiness. Put on the leaf masks and intensify the objective rustling. Only when shaken by deep feeling will you see clearly. Form is law and law is great, it will raise you up. The sky is great. The village is great. Eternal peace is possible. Listen to the caravan music. Follow the all-penetrating, all-encompassing, all-exalting sound. Lift yourselves up. Gauging and knowing, move heavenwards. See the pulse dance of the sun and trust your seething heart. The quivering of your eyelids is the quivering of the truth. Let colours glow. Let this dramatic poem be your guide. Go for ever towards. Take the long way round.

She climbs down from the ladder and comes through the arch with a crown in her hand. She goes to THE CHILD *and indicates with gestures that he should sit down in the hollow.* THE CHILD *does so.* NOVA *puts the crown on his head. The others group themselves round* THE CHILD *and put on the leaf masks. Caravan music.*